SOME MYTHS AND LEGENDS OF THE AUSTRALIAN ABORIGINES

BY

W. J. THOMAS

British Library Cataloguing-in-Publication Data

A catalogue record for this book is available from
the British Library

CONTENTS

"*Tatkanna seized a fire-stick and made off.*"

INTRODUCTION

When the white man first carried the burden and blessing of civilization to the shores of Australia, he found the land inhabited by a very primitive race of people. They lived simple lives, and their activities were confined to hunting, fishing and the procuring of vegetable food. Their dwelling place or gunyah was a rude shelter formed by the boughs and bark of trees, which afforded them little protection from the elements. The weapons of war and the chase used by the men were the boomerang, spear and club. They also used a stone axe, which consisted of a piece of hard brittle stone chipped or ground to a suitable shape and fixed securely in a forked piece of wood by means of bark, string and gum, or animal tendons. The women used a stick hardened by fire and pointed at one end. It was called a "digging stick," and was used both as a weapon and a domestic implement for digging edible roots.

Fish were either speared or caught in nets woven of grass and bark. The nets were set in shallow portions of the river course, and the fish were usually trapped as they travelled with the tides. Extraordinary skill was developed by the natives in the use of the fish spear. The native fisherman would wade in the river and secure his meal by throwing the spear at a ripple in the water which experience had taught him was an indication of the presence of fish.

The kangaroo and other animals were stalked by the blackfellow and killed for food, and the skins and furs were used for sleeping rugs. Certain species of grubs and snakes were included in the somewhat extensive menu of the natives, and, when a lizard was seen basking in the sun, it was promptly caught, cooked and eaten. As the natives had but little knowledge of the methods for preserving animal food, their existence alternated between a feast and a famine. When a big haul of fish was secured, it was customary for them to camp on the riverside until the food supply was exhausted.

The natives lived together in tribes. Each tribe was distinguished by a common language, peculiar tribal customs, burial ceremonies, initiation rites ("man-making"), and magical beliefs. The ceremonies connected with the "making of men" were very elaborate and surrounded with religious secrecy. The secrets of initiation were held exclusively by the men of the tribe, and, if a woman was caught within sight of the ceremonies, she was immediately killed. Attached to each tribe were primitive doctors or "medicine men." These men were supposed to possess methods of magic whereby they could cure disease, heal wounds, bring secret death to members of hostile tribes, make rain in time of drought, and perform other miracles. The natives believed in the power of these men to a degree that is almost incredible to us.

To-day, the living descendants of this primitive native race are the tribes of blackfellows who roam across the northern and central portions of Australia. They live in the same wild state as their forefathers did many centuries before the boom of the white man's gun broke the stillness of their hunting grounds. At one time scientists were agreed in placing the Australian aborigines among the lowest surviving representatives of the human family. They regarded them as the bottom rung in the ladder of civilization.

More recent investigators, however, concur in the opinion that this view is not quite correct; for, though our aborigines are inferior to the ancient Incas of Peru and to most branches of the Polynesian race, they have a remarkable knowledge of Nature, a complex social system, and, where unpolluted by contact with degraded white men, a high moral sense.

The mind of a savage, like that of a child, is filled with a questioning fear of those things which it does not understand. The wonders of Nature, explained so clearly to us by modern science, remain for him a hidden mystery. The impression which he receives from his immediate surroundings is reasoned in the terms of his limited experience and imagination. In this manner, many beautiful myths and legends have been invented by primitive people to explain to their own mental satisfaction the wonderful and terrible natural system of which they are an inseparable part.

The blackfellow, wandering through the dark virgin forest and over the wooded hills, wondered at the mysteries of nature which surrounded him. He saw the warm sun rise from behind the mountains in the east, travel across the blue vault of the sky, and again sink beneath the earth far to the west. When the shadow of night was across the land, he slept beneath a canopy of clouds whose dimness was lit by the light of the moon and studded with golden stars.

In fern-grown gullies, he heard the music of running water as the tiny creek rippled over its stony bed. From the hills, he saw the silver river winding its way through rocky mountain gorges to the distant sea. The flood waters, sweeping down from the snow-capped mountains, were a living thing of terror. With a deep, sullen roar, they carried all before them, and Death followed swiftly on their turbulent tides. Far in the distance the sea glinted like fire in the noon-day sun. Men told strange tales of the sea and the dark, frowning cliffs that guarded the land, while the green surf, carrying with it strange treasures of the deep, thundered on the golden beaches.

The sky was the dwelling place of spirit men who caused the face of the sun to grow dark, the purple shadows to creep across the hills, and the rain to patter softly through the trees. When the white clouds gathered, the wind sang softly through the reeds, like a voice mourning the dead, or howled eerily through the trees in the forest. The voice of the thunder, echoing through the mountain hollows, and the lightning, flashing its golden fire across the sky, caused him to crouch in terror lest the wrath of the storm-god should fall heavily upon him. The unfathomable secret of life and death was ever before him. To the silent wonder of death was added the beautiful gift of dreams-that magic mirror of sleep wherein he saw men long since dead, and lived again in the dim remembered land of the past.

With child-like wonder he heard the song of the bush,

the laugh of the kookaburra greeting the dawn of a new day, and the mournful notes of the night birds betokening its close. When the warm breath of spring woke the sleeping spirit of the bush, she covered the land with a flower-woven covering of scarlet and gold, soft green and purple, like a silken tapestry fallen from the loom of the sun. The wild bees droned drowsily in the noon day, and carried their honey to a nest in some tall gum tree. All the bush echoed with the song of life.

In order to explain the bountiful gifts of Nature in this fairyland of the Australian Bush, the blackfellows invented the beautiful myths and legends which I am about to relate to you.

"Byama threw a spear with all his strength"

THE STORY OF THE SEVEN SISTERS AND THE FAITHFUL LOVERS

In the dream time, many ages ago, the cluster of stars which we now know as the Pleiades, or the Seven Sisters, were seven beautiful ice maidens. Their parents were a great rugged mountain whose dark head was hidden in the clouds, and an ice-cold stream that flowed from the snow-clad hills. The Seven Sisters wandered across the land, with their long hair flying behind them like storm clouds before the breeze. Their cheeks were flushed with the kiss of the sun, and in their eyes was hidden the soft, grey light of the dawn. So entrancing was their beauty, that all men loved them, but the maidens' affections were as cold as the stream which gave them birth, and they never turned aside in their wanderings to gladden the hearts of men.

One day a man named Wurrunnah, by a cunning device, captured two of the maidens, and forced them to live with him, while their five sisters travelled to their home in the sky. When Wurrunnah discovered that the sisters whom he had captured were ice-maidens, whose beautiful tresses were like the icicles that drooped from the trees in winter time, he was disappointed. So he took them to a camp fire, and endeavored to melt the cold crystals from their beautiful limbs. But, as the ice melted, the water quenched the fire, and he succeeded only in dimming their icy brightness.

The two sisters were very lonely and sad in their captivity, and longed for their home in the clear blue sky. When the shadow of night was over the land, they could see their five sisters beckoning to them as they twinkled afar off. One day Wurrunnah told them to gather pine-bark in the forest. After a short journey, they came to a great pine tree, and commenced to strip the bark from it. As they did so, the pine tree (which belonged to the same totem as the maidens) extended itself to the sky. The maidens took advantage of this friendly act, and climbed to the home of their sisters. But they never regained their original brightness, and that is the reason why there are five bright stars and two dim ones in the group of the Pleiades. The Seven Sisters have not forgotten the earth folk. When the snow falls softly they loose their wonderful tresses to the caress of the breeze, to remind us of their journey across our land.

When the Seven Sisters were on earth, of all the men who loved them the Berai Berai, or two brothers, were the most faithful. When they hunted in the forest, or waited in the tall reeds for the wild ducks, they always brought the choicest morsels of the chase as an offering to the Sisters. When the maidens wandered far across the mountains, the Berai Berai followed them, but their love was not favored.

When the maidens set out on their long journey to the sky, the Berai Berai were grieved, and said: "Long have we loved you and followed in your foot steps, O maidens of the dawn, and, when you have left us' we will hunt no more." And they laid aside their weapons and mourned for the maidens until the dark shadow of death fell upon them. When they died, the fairies pitied them, and placed them in the sky, where they could hear the Sisters singing. Thus were they happily rewarded for their constancy. On a starry night, you will see them listening to the song of the Seven Sisters. We call them Orion's Sword and Belt, but it is a happier thought to remember them as the faithful lovers who have listened to the song of the stars from the birth of time.

A LEGEND OF THE SACRED BULLROARER

The Bullroarer is a primitive instrument used by the aborigines at initiation and other ceremonies. It is a thin oblong section of wood, attached to a length of string through a hole at one end. When it is swung rapidly through the air it produces a peculiar humming sound. It is held in sacred veneration by the blacks, and is never seen by the women of the tribe under penalty of death.

In a rocky place in the mountains there lived two brothers named Byama. They were both married, and each man's wife had a son named Weerooimbrall. One day the brothers, accompanied by their wives and other members of the tribe, went far into the forest in search of food. They left the children alone in the camp to await their return.

Close to the camp there lived a bad man named Thoorkook, who had a number of very savage dogs. So terrible were these animals that no man dared to approach them. Thoorkook hated the brothers Byama, and was always planning to injure them. Through the trees he watched them going to the hunt, and his thoughts were evil. Some time later he heard the laughter of the boys at play in the camp, and, as he listened, a terrible thought was born in his wicked mind. He would wreak his vengeance on the brothers by killing their children, whom they loved more than life.

With this intention he loosed the dogs and sent them to the camp. When the brothers and their wives returned to the camp, they were surprised to notice that the children did not run to meet them as they usually did, and that no sound could be heard.

The elder brother said: "I cannot hear the voices of the children; surely they have not wandered into the forest alone; they will be lost. The wild dog; will eat them, or they will die of thirst."

But the other brother laughingly replied: "No. We have hunted far to-day; when we left the camp the breath of night was on the trees, and now the sun is growing cold. They have grown weary with waiting and have fallen asleep. We will find them together like two little possums." When the brothers entered the camp, they found the two little boys lying very cold and still. They called to them, but the boys did not answer-they were dead. And by the marks on their bodies, the brothers knew that they had been killed by Thoorkook's dogs. When the women saw their dead children, they were moved by a frantic grief that was heart-rending to behold, and, all through the night, could be heard the sound of their wailing.

Giant Kangaroos.

Next day, the brothers changed themselves into giant kangaroos, and decided to kill Thoorkook and his savage dogs. They hopped about in sight of Thoorkook's camp, and, when the dogs scented them, they gave chase. With great bounds the kangaroos hopped away, and the dogs followed, but one ran faster than the rest. When it was a long way from the pack, the kangaroos turned, and one of them struck the dog a heavy blow with its paw, which ripped the body from head to tail. They then carried the body and threw it in a deep water hole.

The kangaroos continued to hop away, and the dogs followed fast; red foam flecked their mouths and lolling tongues, the cruel white fangs glistened in the sun, their lean sides panted, and the noise of their deep, hoarse barking echoed through the bush like distant thunder. One dog again ran faster than the rest in this relentless chase. The kangaroos ran slower, as though they were growing tired, and, when the leading dog came within striking distance, they suddenly turned, and, with one swift stroke, ripped it from end to end. This terrible hunt continued until one by one the dogs were killed.

The kangaroos again changed themselves into men and went to Thoorkook's camp to kill him. When he saw them approaching he seized his weapons and prepared to fight. They, however, made the sign of peace by placing their spears in the ground, and he did likewise.

The elder brother then spoke to him, saying: "While we were hunting, you crawled like an adder in the grass and killed our children with your dogs. We have killed your dogs, and the crows are whitening their bones. I am now going to kill you, not as you kill children, but as men kill men, and, when you are dead, I will change you into a bird that will live forever in the darkness of night, and never see the sun."

Thoorkook did not answer; he knew that he would have to fight for his life. Picking up his spears and a wooden shield, he followed Byama to a clear space in the bush where the trial of skill was to take place.

The Great Fight.

The two men stood facing each other some distance apart; each held a long spear poised for throwing in one hand, while in the other was held a wooden shield which partly covered his body. At a given signal from the younger brother the fight commenced. The spears flew through the air like beams of light, and their long shafts quivered as they missed their mark, and buried deep in the trees.

Both the men were very skilled spear-throwers, and the fight was a long one. No sound was heard except the hissing of the spears in flight, the heavy breathing of the men, who were tired through their great exertions, and the dull thud of their feet on the grass as they leapt forward. In a desperate effort to end the fight, Byama threw a spear at his enemy's throat with all his strength. Thoorkook saw it coming, and instantly raised his shield to guard himself. The spear was hurled with such force, however, that it pierced the wooden shield, entered Thoorkook's throat, and came out on the other side.

At the death of their enemy, the brothers rejoiced, and, before leaving for their camp, they turned his body into a Mopoke, a dismal night bird with a very harsh cry. When they returned to their camp the brothers found that the mothers of the dead boys would not cease crying, and they were so moved with pity at the women's grief that they turned them into Curlews. When you hear the mournful cry of the Curlews in the bush, you will know it is the mothers crying for their little boys they lost so long ago.

The Flying Chip.

One day the brothers were out hunting. The younger brother had climbed a tree, and -was cutting out a white wood grub, when a chip from his axe went whizzing through the air and fell near the elder brother, who was standing at the foot of the tree. When Byama descended the tree, his brother suggested that they should go hunting in different directions for the remainder of the day. Byama agreed to the proposal and went his way. The elder brother was then left alone. He carefully cut a thin piece of wood like the chip, and tied a piece of bark string to one end of it, and, when he swung it through the air, it made the same sound as the flying chip.

He continued his hunting, and, when he returned to the camp at the close of the day, he showed the piece of wood to his brother and said: "The voices of our children dwell in the trees, and, though we cannot see them, they will be with us for ever." The younger brother feared that he had lost his reason, and said to him: "You have travelled far to-day, and the fires of the sun burned brightly; you must be very tired. Sleep, my brother, and when the new day dawns you will feel better, and then we will talk." Seeing he could not convince his younger brother, Byama went into the open and swung the piece of wood, and the low, soft sound that rose and fell was like the voice of the little children.

The two brothers--who were headmen of their tribes-- then decided that this piece of wood, which is called the Bullroarer, should be shown to all boys born in the future, in remembrance of the little boys who were killed by the dogs. And even to the present day the Curlews cry mournfully in the woods, and the Mopoke only ventures abroad at night.

WHY THE WHALE SPOUTS,
THE STARFISH IS RAGGED, AND THE
NATIVE BEAR HAS STRONG ARMS

Many years ago, when this old world was young, all the animals now living in Australia were men.

At that time, they lived in a distant land across the ocean, and, having heard of the wonderful hunting grounds in Australia, they determined to leave their country and sail to this sunny land in a canoe. They knew that the voyage would be a long and dangerous one; storms would sweep across the sea and lash the waves into a white fury; the wind would howl like the evil spirits of the forest, the lightning flash across the sky like writhing golden snakes, and death would hide in waiting for them beneath the brown sea kelp. It was therefore necessary for them to have a very strong canoe for the journey.

The whale, who was the biggest of all the men, had a great strong canoe that could weather the wildest storm. But he was a very selfish fellow and would not allow anybody the use of it. As it was necessary to have the canoe, his companions watched for a suitable opportunity to steal it and start on their long and lonely journey. But the whale was a cunning creature. He always kept very strict guard over the canoe and would not leave it alone for a moment. The other people were at their wits' end to solve the problem of stealing the canoe, and, as a last resource, they held a great council to consider the question. Many suggestions were put forward, but none was practical. It seemed an impossible task, until the starfish came forward to place his suggestion before the council.

Now, the starfish was a very intimate friend of the whale, so, when he spoke, everybody was very silent and attentive. He hesitated for a moment, and then said:

"Unless we get a very big canoe, it will be impossible to sail to the new hunting-grounds, where the fire of the sun never dies, the sea sand is soft and golden, and there is plenty of food. I shall get my friend, the whale, to leave his canoe and I shall keep him interested for a long time. When I give you the signal, steal silently away with it as fast as you can."

The other men were so excited at the proposal that they all spoke at once and asked: "How will you do it?" But the starfish looked very wise and said, "Your business is to steal the canoe and mine to keep the whale occupied while you do it."

Some days later the starfish paid a friendly visit to the whale, and, after talking for some time, he said, "I have noticed what a great number of vermin you have in your hair. They must be very uncomfortable. Let me catch them for you."

The whale being greatly troubled with vermin in his head, readily agreed to the kind offer of his friend, the starfish. The whale moored his canoe in deep water and sat on a rock. Starfish placed his friend's head in his lap and proceeded to hunt diligently for the vermin. While he was doing so, he told many funny stories and occupied the attention of the whale. The starfish then gave the signal to the men who were waiting, and they seized the canoe and sailed off.

But the whale was very suspicious. For a short time he would forget his canoe, but then he would suddenly remember it and say: "Is my canoe all right?" The starfish had cunningly provided himself with a piece of bark, and, tapping it on the rock in imitation of the boat bumping with the rise and fall of the sea, he would answer, "Yes, this is it I am tapping with my hand. It is a very fine canoe."

He continued to tell funny stories to the whale. At the same time, he scratched very hard around his ears in order to silence the sound of the oars splashing in the water as the other men rowed away with the canoe. After some time, the whale grew tired of his friend's attention and story-telling, and decided to have a look at the canoe himself. When he looked around and found the canoe missing, he could hardly believe it. He rubbed his eyes and looked again. Away in the distance, he could see the vanishing shape of his canoe. Then the truth dawned upon him-he had been tricked.

The whale was very angry and beat the starfish unmercifully. Throwing him upon the rocks, he made great ragged cuts in the faithless creature. The starfish was so exhausted, that he rolled off the rocks and hid himself in the soft sand. It is on account of this cruel beating that, even to the present day, the starfish has a very ragged and torn appearance, and always hides himself in the sand.

After beating the friend who had betrayed him, the whale jumped into the water and chased the men in the canoe. Great white waves rose and fell, as he churned his way through the water, and, out of a wound in his head which the starfish had made, he spouted water high into the air.

The whale continued his relentless chase, and, when the men in the canoe saw him, they said, "He is gaining on us, and, when he catches us, we shall all be drowned." But the native bear, who was in charge of the oars, said, "There is no need to be afraid; look at my arms. They are strong enough to row the canoe out of danger." This reassured his companions, and the chase continued.

The voyage lasted many days and nights. During the day, the hot sun beat down on the men in the canoe, and, at night, the cold winds chilled them. But there was no escape; they must go on. By day and night, they could see the whale spouting in his fury, and churning the sea into foam with the lashing of his tail.

At last land was sighted, and the men rowed very fast towards it. When they landed from the canoe, they were very weary, and sat down on the sand to rest. But the native companion, who was always a very lively fellow and fond of dancing, danced upon the bottom of the canoe until he made a hole in it. He then pushed it a short distance from the shore, where it settled down in the water -and became the small island that is now at the entrance of Lake Illawarra.

When the whale arrived at the landing place, he saw the

men on shore and his canoe wrecked. He travelled along the coast and spouted water with anger as he thought of the trick that had been played on him, and of the wreck of his beloved canoe.

Even to the present day whales spout, the starfish is ragged and torn, the native bear has very strong fore paws, and the blackfellow still roams across the wild wastes of Australia.

A LEGEND OF THE GREAT FLOOD

In the dream-time, a terrible drought swept across the land. The leaves of the trees turned brown and fell from the branches, the flowers drooped their heads and died, and the green grass withered as though the spirit from the barren mountain had breathed upon it with a breath of fire. When the hot wind blew, the dead reeds rattled in the river bed, and the burning sands shimmered like a silver lagoon.

All the water had left the rippling creeks, and deep, still water holes. In the clear blue sky the sun was a mass of molten gold; the clouds no longer drifted across the hills, and the only darkness that fell across the land was the shadow of night and death.

After many had died of thirst, all the animals in the land met together in a great council to discover the cause of the drought. They travelled many miles. Some came from the bush, and others from the distant mountains.

The sea-birds left their homes in the cliffs where the white surf thundered, and flew without resting many days and nights. When they all arrived at the chosen meeting place in Central Australia, they discovered that a frog of enormous size had swallowed all the water in the land, and thus caused the drought. After much serious discussion, it was decided that the only way to obtain the water again was to make the frog laugh. The question now arose as to which animal should begin the performance, and, after a heated argument, the pride of place was given to the Kookaburra.

The animals then formed themselves into a huge circle with the frog in the centre. Red kangaroos, grey wallaroos, rock and swamp wallabies, kangaroo rats, bandicoots, native bears and ring-tailed possums all sat together. The emu and the native companion forgot their quarrel and the bell bird his chimes. Even a butcher bird looked pleasantly at a brown snake, and the porcupine forgot to bristle. A truce had been called in the war of the bush.

Now, the Kookaburra, seated himself on the limb of a tree, and, with a wicked twinkle in his eye, looked straight at the big, bloated frog, ruffled his brown feathers, and began to laugh. At first, he made a low gurgling sound deep in his throat, as though he was smiling to himself, but gradually he raised his voice and laughed louder and louder until the bush re-echoed with the sound of his merriment. The other animals looked on with very serious faces, but the frog gave no sign. He just blinked his eyes and looked as stupid as only a frog can look.

The Kookaburra continued to laugh until he nearly choked and fell off the tree, but all without success. The next competitor was a frill-lizard. It extended the frill around its throat, and, puffing out its jaws, capered up and down. But there was no humor in the frog; he did not even look at the lizard, and laughter was out of the question. It was then suggested that the dancing of the native companion might tickle the fancy of the frog. So the native companion danced until she was tired, but all her graceful and grotesque figures failed to arouse the interest of the frog.

The position was very serious, and the council of animals was at its wits' end for a reasonable suggestion. In their anxiety to solve the difficulty, they all spoke at once, and the din was indescribable. Above the noise could be heard a frantic cry of distress. A carpet snake was endeavoring to swallow a porcupine. The bristles had stuck in his throat, and a kookaburra, who had a firm grip of his tail, was making an effort to fly away with him.

Close by, two bandicoots were fighting over the possession of a sweet root, but, while they were busily engaged in scratching each other, a possum stole it. They then forgot their quarrel and chased the possum, who escaped danger by climbing a tree and swinging from a branch by his tail. In this peculiar position he ate the root at his leisure, much to the disgust of the bandicoots below.

After peace and quiet had been restored, the question of the drought was again considered. A big eel, who lived in a deep water hole in the river, suggested that he should be given an opportunity of making the frog laugh. Many of the animals laughed at the idea, but, in despair, they agreed to give him a trial. The eel then began to wriggle in front of the frog. At first he wriggled slowly, then faster and faster until his head and tail met. Then he slowed down and wriggled like a snake with the shivers. After a few minutes, he changed his position, and flopped about like a well-bitten grub on an ant bed.

The frog opened his sleepy eyes, his big body quivered,

his face relaxed, and, at last, he burst into a laugh that sounded like rolling thunder. The water poured from his mouth in a flood. It filled the deepest rivers and covered the land. Only the highest mountain peaks were visible, like islands in the sea. Many men and animals were drowned.

The pelican-who was a blackfellow at this time -sailed from island to island in a great canoe and rescued any blackfellow he saw. At last he came to an island on which there were many people. In their midst he saw a beautiful woman, and f ell in love with her. He rescued all the men on this island until the woman alone remained. Every time he made a journey she would ask him to take her with the men, but he would reply: "There are many in the canoe. I will carry you next time." He did this several times, and at last the woman guessed that he was going to take her to his camp. She then determined to escape from the pelican. While he was away, she wrapped a log in her possum rug, and placed it near the gunyah; then, as the flood was subsiding, she escaped to the bush. When he returned, he called to her, but, receiving no answer, he walked over to the possum rug and touched it with his foot. It, however, did not move. He then tore the rug away from what he supposed was a woman, but, when he found a log, he was very angry, and resolved to be revenged. He painted himself with white clay, and set out to look for the other blackfellows, with the intention of killing them. But the first pelican he met was so frightened by his strange appearance, that it struck him with a club and killed him. Since that time pelicans have been black and white in remembrance of the Great Flood.

The flood gradually subsided, and the land was again clothed in the green garments of spring. Through the tall green reeds the voice of the night wind whispered soft music to the river. And, when the dawn came from the eastern sky, the birds sang a song of welcome to the new flood-a flood of golden sunlight.

"Rolla-Mano determined to capture them"

HOW THE STARS WERE MADE

Rolla-Mano and the Evening Star.

Rolla-Mano was the old man of the sea. The blue ocean, with all its wonderful treasures of glistening pearls, white foam and pink coral, belonged to him. In the depths of the sea, he ruled a kingdom of shadows and strange forms, to which the light of the sun descended in green and grey beams. The forests of this weird land were many trees of brown sea-kelp, whose long arms waved slowly to and fro with the ebb and flow of the water. Here and there were patches of sea grass, fine and soft as a snow maiden's hair. In the shadow of the trees lurked a thousand terrors of the deep. In a dark rocky cave, a giant octopus spread its long, writhing tentacles in search of its prey, and gazed the while through the water with large lustreless eyes. In and out of the kelp a grey shark swam swiftly and without apparent motion, while bright-colored fish darted out of the path of danger. Across the rippled sand a great crab ambled awkwardly to its hiding place behind a white-fluted clam shell. And over all waved the long, brown arms of the sea kelp forest. Such was the kingdom of Rolla-Mano, the old man of the sea.

One day Rolla-Mano went to fish in a lonely mangrove

swamp close to the sea shore. He caught many fish, and cooked them at a fire. While eating his meal he noticed two women approach him. Their beautiful bodies were as lithe and graceful as the wattle tree, and in their eyes was the soft light of the dusk. When they spoke, their voices were as sweet and low as the sighing of the night breeze through the reeds in the river. Rolla-Mano determined to capture them. With this intention he hid in the branches of the mangrove tree, and, when the women were close to him he threw his net over them. One, however, escaped by diving into the water. He was so enraged at her escape that he jumped in after her with a burning fire stick in his hand. As soon as the fire stick touched the water, the sparks hissed and scattered to the sky, where they remain as golden stars to this day.

Rolla-Mano did not capture the woman who dived into the dark waters of the swamp. After a fruitless search he returned to the shore and took the other woman to live with him for ever in the sky. She is the evening star. From her resting place, she gazes through the mists of eternity at the restless sea-the dark, mysterious kingdom of Rolla-Mano. On a clear summer night, when the sky is studded with golden stars, you will remember that they are the sparks from the fire stick of Rolla-Mano, and the beautiful evening star is the woman he captured in the trees of the mangrove swamp.

WHY THE CROW IS BLACK

One day, a crow and a hawk hunted together in the bush. After travelling together for some time, they decided to hunt in opposite directions, and, at the close of the day, to share whatever game they had caught. The crow travelled against the sun, and at noonday arrived at a broad lagoon which was the haunt of the wild ducks. The crow hid in the tall green reeds fringing the lagoon, and prepared to trap the ducks. First, he got some white clay, and, having softened it with water, placed two pieces in his nostrils. He then took a long piece of hollow reed through which he could breathe under water, and finally tied a net bag around his waist in which to place the ducks.

On the still surface of the lagoon, the tall gum trees were reflected like a miniature forest. The ducks, with their bronze plumage glistening in the sun, were swimming among the clumps of reeds, and only paused to dive for a tasty morsel hidden deep in the water weeds. The crow placed the reed in his mouth, and, without making any sound, waded into the water. He quickly submerged himself, and the only indication of his presence in the lagoon, was a piece of dry reed which projected above the surface of the water, and through which the crow was breathing. When he reached the centre of the water hole he remained perfectly still. He did not have to wait long for the ducks to swim above his head. Then, without making any sound or movement, he seized one by the leg, quickly pulled it beneath the water, killed it, and placed it in the net bag. By doing this, he did not frighten the other ducks, and, in a short time he had trapped a number of them. He then left the lagoon and continued on his way until he came to a river.

The crow was so pleased with his success at the waterhole, that he determined to spear some fish before he returned to his camp. He left the bag of ducks on the bank of the river, and, taking his fish spear, he waded into the river until the water reached his waist. Then he stood very still, with the spear poised for throwing. A short distance from the spot where he was standing, a slight ripple disturbed the calm surface of the water. With the keen eye of the hunter, he saw the presence of fish, and, with a swift movement of his arm, he hurled the spear, and his unerring aim was rewarded with a big fish. The water was soon agitated by many fish, and the crow took advantage of this to spear many more. With this heavy load of game, he turned his face towards home.

The hawk was very unfortunate in his hunting. He stalked a kangaroo many miles, and then lost sight of it in the thickly wooded hills. He then decided to try the river for some fish, but the crow had made the water muddy and frightened the fish, so again he was unsuccessful. At last the hawk decided to return to his gunyah with the hope that the crow would secure some food, which they had previously agreed to share. When the hawk arrived, he found that the crow had been there before him and had prepared and eaten his evening meal. He at once noticed that the crow had failed to leave a share for him. This annoyed the hawk, so he approached the crow and said: "I see you have had a good hunt to-day. I walked many miles but could not catch even a lizard. I am tired and would be glad to have my share of food, as we agreed this morning." "You are too lazy," the crow replied. "You must have slept in the sun instead of hunting for food. Anyhow, I've eaten mine and cannot give you any." This made the hawk very angry, and he .attacked the crow. For a long time they struggled around the dying embers of the camp fire, until the hawk seized the crow and rolled him in the black ashes. When the crow recovered from the fight, he found that he could not wash the ashes off, and, since that time, crows have always been black. The crow was also punished for hiding the food which he could not eat by being condemned to live on putrid flesh.

WHY FLYING FOXES HANG FROM TREES

A Legend of the Striped-Tail Lizard.

The Flying Fox and the Striped-tail Lizard were friends. They lived in the same gunyah and hunted together. One day the lizard said: "I will visit a tribe of blacks with whom I am very friendly, and bring back a bundle of spears." The fox was very doubtful about the truth of the lizard's remarks, and said: "I would not like to wait for food until you get the spears." This annoyed the lizard, and, without replying, he set out on his journey. He wandered through the bush all day, but failed to find the blacks. He then followed the winding river for many miles, but without success. Towards nightfall, a storm swept down from the mountains; the wind howled eerily through the swaying trees, and the rain fell in torrents. The lizard was in a sorry plight. Weary and wet, he wandered through the bush and at last arrived at his gunyah. The door was closed, and, when he asked the fox to open it, the fox asked a question. "Have you any spears with you?" he called. Now the lizard knew that if the fox was aware of his unsuccessful journey, he would make great fun of it, so he replied: "I have a big bundle of spears. I met my friends at the in the land that lies beyond the sunset. Many dangers are there, O my brother. The evil spirits sing soft and low through the trees, like the voice of a maiden calling to her lover, and he who follows the sound of the voices goes on for ever, and never returns. The great Black Bat waits for you in the forest. You are weary with your long journey. Stay with us and rest you awhile; then you can return to your tribe."

Yoonecara was very pleased with the friendly reception he received, but he could not be dissuaded from his journey, and, after bidding them farewell, he continued on his way. Through the trees he could hear the voices of the Dheeyabry people calling to him to return, but he would not heed them. As he journeyed on, the voices grew fainter and fainter until they were lost in the great silence.

After leaving the Dheeyabry, Yoonecara travelled many days and arrived at a place where the March flies and mosquitoes were larger and more numerous than any he had seen before. The buzzing of the mosquitoes was like the sound of the bullroarer. They attacked him savagely, and, try as he would, he could not escape them. When he attempted to sleep, they settled on him in swarms and tormented him with their stings. In desperation, Yoonecara sat by a waterhole and built a fire. Then he considered his dangerous position. "If I cannot protect myself from these insects," he reflected, "my bones will soon be gleaming white in the sun. I have travelled far, but the journey is beyond the strength of man. I will return to my tribe." These were the thoughts passing through his mind. He then considered ways and means whereby he could protect himself against the mosquitoes, and at last discovered an excellent plan. He stripped a sheet of bark from a tree. It was as long as himself and of sufficient width to enclose his body. After tying bushes around his ankles and head, he doubled the bark around his body. With this protection, he journeyed through the Land of the Giant Mosquitoes. And, when he had no further use for his covering of bark he placed it in a waterhole in order to keep it soft, that he might use it on his return journey. After he had braved this danger, his courage returned, and he travelled on.

For some time, his journey was without adventure, but one day he came to the edge of a great boggy marsh known as Kolliworoogla. At the sight of this marsh, he thought further progress was impossible. After carefully examining the edge of the swamp, he discovered what appeared to be the trunk of a fallen tree that lay across it. He ventured along this dangerous bridge and safely reached the far side of the swamp. He then came to a place where there was a very high rock, which was hollowed out on one side like a cave. On approaching it, he found that it was a cave, and in it he could see his ancestor Byama, asleep. At last, Yoonecara had reached his long journey's end. Byama was a man of giant proportions-much bigger than the blackfellows of the present time. At the front of the cave, one of Byama's daughters, Byallaburragan, was sitting at a fire roasting a carpet snake. She offered a portion to the traveller, and said: "Long and weary has been your journey, O faithful one, and many the dangers that crossed your path. Like the light of the sun was the fire of your courage, and this shall be your reward. Your name shall be passed through the ages on the tongues of our people. You shall be honored as the only man who travelled to the home of Byama, and returned; for no man shall ever do the like again."

Around Byama's dwelling the country was very beautiful, and was a dream of delight to the weary traveller. The tall, green trees leaned towards the cave, and their leafy branches gave cool shade on the hottest day, while the song of the birds at sunset was like a mother crooning her baby to sleep. The grass grew high on the plains, and, when the wind blew, it billowed like the waves of the sea. In front of the cave, a stream of water, clear as crystal, ran its course to a deep lagoon. The water of the lagoon teemed with fish, and in the reeds, there were many ducks, swans, and other water-fowl.

After he had rested for some time in this pleasant land, Yoonecara returned to his own tribe and related his wonderful experiences. Soon after his return he died, and, since that time, no man has travelled to the Land of the Setting Sun.

*"When the strange-looking blackfellows were close to him,
Yoonecara released the bandicoot"*

WHY BLACKFELLOWS NEVER TRAVEL ALONE

A Legend of the Wallaroo and Willy-Wagtail

Alone, on a rocky ridge high in the mountains, a wallaroo made his camping-ground beneath the shady boughs of a mountain ash. He was very old and infirm, and too weak to hunt for food, so he sat by his camp fire all the day and lashed the ground with his strong tail. The low, rhythmic thud-thud-thud of its beating could be heard above the song of the birds. One day a paddymelon was passing close by the camp when he heard the beating of the wallaroo's tail. After following the direction of the sound, he came to the camp, and asked the wallaroo if he was in trouble. "I am very sick," the wallaroo replied. "Many times have I seen the snow on the mountains, and I am growing too old to hunt. My brothers have gone to the river beyond the hills to spear fish for me, but they have not returned, and I am very hungry." The paddymelon was sorry for the old wallaroo, and offered to go to the river in search of the fishermen. He walked a short distance from the camp when the wallaroo, called after him: "You had better take my boomerang with you, as you may meet some game on your way." The paddymelon turned

41

around and said: "All right, I shall take it. Throw it to me!" The crafty wallaroo picked up the boomerang, and, taking careful aim, threw it with all his strength. It struck the unfortunate paddymelon a terrible blow and killed him. The wallaroo took the fur from the dead animal and prepared the body for cooking. He dug a hole in the ground, lined it with stones, placed the meat in it, and covered it with flat stones. He then built a fire over it, and in a short time had cooked a tasty meal.

When the paddymelon did not return home, his relatives became very anxious about him. At last an iguana offered to go in search of the missing member of the tribe. He followed the tracks of the paddymelon through the bush, and they led to the camp of the wallaroo. When the iguana approached the camp the wallaroo was beating his tail on the ground. The iguana asked him if he needed any assistance, and, in a plaintive voice, the wallaroo told him the same tale that had been told to the unlucky paddymelon. The iguana was sorry for the old wallaroo, and offered to seek his relatives for him and tell them of his plight. When he turned to go, the wallaroo asked him if he would take a spear with him in case he met with any game on his way. The iguana said, "I will take it; throw it to me." The wallaroo had been waiting for this opportunity, and he hurled the spear so swiftly that it transfixed the iguana before he could jump aside. The wallaroo then prepared another meal as before.

One day passed, and yet another, but the iguana did not return to the hunting ground of his tribe. They sent a bandicoot in search of the iguana, but he met the same fate at the hands of the wallaroo. After waiting anxiously for the return of the bandicoot, the head-men of the tribe called a great council. When all the members were assembled together a headman said: "Many moons ago our brother the paddymelon left the camp before the sun was over the hills, and when night came he did not return, and his shadow has not darkened the ground for many days. The iguana went in search of him. He is a great hunter, but he has not returned. Yesterday the bandicoot followed in their tracks, but I fear the shadow of death has fallen over them. We must find them." Many suggestions were placed before the council, but none of them seemed practical. Then the willy-wagtail, who was a clever medicine man, spoke: "Long have we waited for the return of our brothers, and yet we do not hear their call. I shall follow their footsteps even to the shadowy hunting ground of death, but I shall return to you." The council consented to the willy-wagtail's proposal, but they were afraid that he would walk to the Land of Silence and never return.

Before dawn the willy-wagtail started on his dangerous and lonely journey. When he reached the summit of the mountain, he could see, far in the distance, the grey smoke of the camp fires wreathing slowly above the trees. With a sad but brave heart he continued his journey. After travelling for some time he heard the sound of the wallaroo beating his tail on the ground. At first he thought it was a wallaroo hopping through the bush, but, as the sound did not grow louder or fainter, he became suspicious, and approached the camp very cautiously. The wallaroo saw him approaching, and, calling to him, told him the same story as before. The willy-wagtail offered to seek his relatives for him, and, with this intention, started on his way. When he had gone a short distance the wallaroo offered him a boomerang. The willy-wagtail was very suspicious about his intention, and said: "Throw it to me; it will save me the trouble of walking back to the tree."

The wallaroo then threw the weapon with all his strength, but the willy-wagtail was prepared, and, as soon as the boomerang left the hand of the thrower, he jumped quickly aside. When the wallaroo saw he had missed his mark, and that his evil intentions were known to the willy-wagtail, he became furious, and threw all his spears and nullanullas at him, but failed to strike him. Then the willy-wagtail took the boomerang and threw it at the old wallaroo. It struck him a heavy blow on the chest and killed him. He then skinned him, and prepared to cook his flesh, but he was too old and tough to eat. He now took the skin and returned to the camp. When he told the tribe of the fate of their brothers they were sorely grieved, but their grief was turned to joy when the willy-wagtail showed them the skin of their enemy. The wagtail was rewarded by being made a headman of the tribe.

The headmen now decided that blackfellows should never travel alone. As a mark of remembrance, wallaroos have always had a strip of white fur on their breasts. It is an indication of the boomerang wound that killed the old wallaroo of Mountain Ridge.

HOW THE KANGAROO GOT A LONG TAIL, AND THE WOMBAT A FLAT FOREHEAD

Many years ago, Mirram the kangaroo and Warreen the wombat were both men. They were very friendly, and hunted and lived together in the same camping-ground. Warreen had a very comfortable gunyah made of bark and soft leaves, but Mirram who was a careless fellow-did not trouble to build a home. He was content to sleep in the open, by the side of a big fire, with the blue sky for a cover, and the green grass for a couch. This open air life was very nice in fine weather, when the stars twinkled in the sky like golden fire-flies, but it was extremely uncomfortable in the rainy season.

Ore night a great storm arose. The wind howled eerily, and rocked the tall trees to and fro as though they were shaken by the strong arms of an invisible giant. The rain fell in torrents, and darkness covered the light of the stars. The rain quickly quenched the glowing embers of Mirram's fire, and he was left to the mercy of the storm. After shivering in the cold for some time, he decided to seek the hospitality of Warreen. "Surely my friend would not refuse me shelter on such a night as this," he thought. "I will ask him."

Feeling very cold and miserable, he crept to the

opening of Warreen's tent, and seeing there was sufficient space for both of them to sleep comfortably, he woke him and said: "The storm has killed my fire. I am very wet, and the cold wind has chilled me to the bone. May I sleep in the corner of your tent?" Warreen blinked his eyes sleepily and answered in a gruff voice: "No. I want to place my head in that corner. There isn't any room." With this rude remark he moved into the corner, but, as he could not occupy the whole space of the tent, another corner became vacant. Mirram went away and sat by the wet ashes of his fire, and his thoughts were as miserable as the weather. The fury of the storm increased, and looking anxiously at the rainproof gunyah of his friend, he decided to approach Warreen again. He entered the shelter, and, touching Warreen gently on the shoulder, said: "The wind is very cold, and as biting as the teeth of the wild dog. The rain is falling heavily and will not cease. I should be grateful if you would allow me to sleep in that corner. I will not disturb you." Warreen raised his head, listened to the moaning of the storm outside, and then replied: "I will not have you here; there isn't any room. Go outside and do not keep waking me." "But," replied Mirram, "there is room in that corner. Surely you wouldn't drive me out into the storm to die!"

Thereupon, Warreen moved one leg into the corner and again a space became vacant. Seeing he could no longer hoodwink Mirram and hide from him his selfish intentions, he grew very angry and yelled: "Get out! Get out! I won't have you in my tent. I don't care where you die." This harsh treatment exasperated Mirram and he left the tent in a terrible rage. Outside the tent, he groped around in the dark until he found a large flat stone. Then he crept silently to the gunyah. By the sound of heavy breathing he knew Warreen was asleep. Moving very silently, he entered the tent, and, raising the stone high in his arms, dashed it on the head of the sleeper. The terrible blow did not kill Warreen but flattened his forehead. When he had recovered from his pained surprise, he heard the mocking voice of Mirram saying: "That is your reward for treating a friend so cruelly. You and your children and their children's children will wander through the land with flat foreheads that men may know them for your selfishness." As Warreen was no match for his opponent, he did not answer, but nursed his sore head and some very bad thoughts. From that moment, he was always planning revenge for his injury.

Some time later, Warreen was hunting in the forest, and, through the shadow of the trees, he saw Mirram a short distance ahead. He crept noiselessly towards him, and, when Mirram was looking for the marks of a possum on the bark of a tree, he threw a spear at him with all his strength. The spear struck Mirram at the bottom of the back, and so deeply did it enter that he could not pull it out. While he was struggling with the spear, Warreen walked up to him, and, in a bantering voice, said: "Aha! My turn has come at last. I have waited long to repay you. You will always carry the spear in your back and wander without a home while you live. Your children will carry the spear and be homeless for ever. By these tokens, men will always remember your attempt to kill me while I slept."

From that time the kangaroo has had a long tail, which makes a low, thudding sound as he wanders homeless through the bush, and the wombat still has a very flat forehead as an everlasting sign of selfishness.

"Mirram crept silently to the gunyah"

49

WHY THE EMU HAS SHORT WINGS
AND THE NATIVE COMPANION
A HARSH VOICE

An emu with very long wings once made her home in the sky. One day she looked over the edge of the clouds, and down on the earth she saw a great gathering of birds dancing by a reed-grown lagoon. High in a gumtree the bell birds were making sweet music with their silvery chimes; the kookaburra, perched on the limb of a dead tree, was chuckling pleasantly to himself; while the native companion danced gracefully on the grass nearby.

The emu was very interested in dancing, so she flew down from her home beyond the clouds, and asked the birds if they would teach her to dance. A cunning old native companion replied: "We shall be very pleased to teach you our dances, but you could never learn with such long wings. If you like, we will clip them for you." The emu did not give much thought to the fact that short wings would never carry her home again. So great was her vanity that she allowed her wings to be clipped very short. When she had done so, the native companions immediately spread their long wings-which they had previously concealed by folding them close against their backs-and flew away, leaving the emu lonely and wiser than before. She never returned to her home in the sky, because her wings would not grow again. They have remained short and useless ever since. This is the reason why emus run very fast, but never fly.

After wandering alone for a long time the emu reconciled herself to a home on the earth, and reared a large family. One day she was walking through the bush when the native companion-who also had a large family-saw her in the distance. The native companion immediately hid all her chicks in the undergrowth, except one; then she approached the emu in a friendly manner, and said: "What a very weary life you must have feeding such a large family. You are looking very ill, and I am sure you will die. I have only one chick. Take my advice and kill your chicks before they kill you." The foolish emu again listened to the soft words of the other bird, and destroyed all her chicks.

Thereupon the native companion called in a low, sweet voice, "Geralka Beralka, Geralka Beralka," and all her fluffy little chicks came running to her from the bushes in which she had hidden them. The emu was frantic with grief when she realised what she had done; but once again she paid the price of vanity and idle flattery with a sad and lonely heart. The native companion was so eager to call her chicks after the cruel trick she had played on the emu that she twisted her neck, and lost her beautiful voice for ever. And now she can call with only two harsh, discordant sounds.

The seasons passed, and once again the emu had a big clutch of eggs. One day the native companion paid her a visit and pretended to be friendly, but the sight of her old enemy made the emu very angry. The emu made a savage rush at her, but the native companion hopped over her back and broke all the eggs except one. After dancing around for a little while, the native companion made a determined rush, and, seizing the remaining egg, threw it up into the sky.

"The Native Companions were dancing."

HOW THE SUN WAS MADE

Dawn, Noontide and Night.

When the emu egg was hurled up to the sky it struck a great pile of wood which had been gathered by a cloud man named Ngoudenout. It hit the wood with such force that the pile instantly burst into flame, and flooded the earth with the soft, warm light of dawn. The flowers were so surprised that they lifted their sleepy heads to the sky, and opened their petals so wide that the glistening dewdrops which night had given them fell to the ground and were lost.

The little birds twittered excitedly on the trees, and the fairies, who kept the snow on the mountain tops, forgot their task, and allowed it to thaw and run into the rivers and creeks. And what was the cause of this excitement?

Away to the east, far over the mountains, the purple shadows of night were turning grey; the soft, pink-tinted clouds floated slowly across the sky like red-breasted birds winging their way to a far land. Along the dim sky-line a path of golden fire marked the parting of the grey shadows, and down in the valley the white mist was hiding the pale face of night.

Like a sleeper stirring softly at the warm touch of a

kiss, all living things of the bush stirred at the caress of dawn. The sun rose with golden splendor in a clear blue sky, and, with its coming, the first day dawned. At first the wood pile burned slowly, but the heat increased, until at noonday it was thoroughly ablaze. But gradually it burnt lower and lower, until at twilight only a heap of glowing embers remained. These embers slowly turned cold and grey. The purple shadows and white mists came from their hiding-places, and once again the mantle of night was over the land.

When Ngoudenout saw what a splendid thing the sun was, he determined to give it to us for ever. At night, when the fire of the sun has burnt out, he goes to a dark forest in the sky and collects a great pile, of wood. At dawn he lights it, and it burns feebly until noonday is reached, then it slowly burns away until twilight and night falls. Ngoudenout, the eternal wood gatherer, then makes his lonely way to the forest for the wood that lights the fire of the sun.

THUGINE, THE RAINBOW AND THE WANDERING BOYS

Far to the west in the deep blue sea there dwells a great serpent named Thugine. His scales are of many shimmering colors. When a rainbow appears in the sky, it is Thugine curving his back and the sun reflecting the colors of his scales.

Many years ago, a tribe of blacks camped close to a sea beach. One morning they all went out to fish and hunt, with the exception of two boys, whom the old men left in charge of the camp. Wander not into the forest lest the wild dogs eat you, or to the beach, where Thugine the serpent is -waiting for children who wander alone." This was the parting advice of the old men to the boys.

When the men had departed, the boys played about the camp for a while, but they soon grew tired of their games. The day was very hot, and in the distance the boys could hear the dull, deep booming of the surf. Both the boys were longing to go to the beach, but were afraid to speak their desire. At last the elder boy spoke, and said: "The fires of the sun are burning bright to-day, but on the breeze I can feel the cool breath of the sea. Let us go to the beach, and we shall return before the shadow of night has fallen. The men will not know." The other boy hesitated and was afraid, but at last he yielded, and together they wandered hand in hand through the bush.

After walking for some time they came to an opening in the trees, and, before their expectant gaze, a wonderful scene unfolded. A golden beach stretched far away until it was lost to view in the dim distance. The cool waves rolled lazily in great green billows from the outer reef, and dashed in a haze of sparkling white foam on the hot sands of the palm-fringed beach. The song of the sea rose in a deep, loud booming, and gradually died away to a low, soft murmuring. The boys were lost in wonder at the beauty of the scene. Never had they seen such an expanse of water sparkling in the sun like the blue sky. Over its rippled surface the shadows ,of the clouds floated like sails across the sun.

Thugine, the serpent, had seen the boys coming from afar, and, while they played on the beach, he swam swiftly and silently to the shore and seized them. When the men arrived at the camp, they discovered the absence of the boys. They searched the bush all through the -night, and at dawn came to the beach. Far from the shore they saw two, black rocks jutting out of the sea. Then they knew that Thugine had taken the wandering boys and turned them into rocks. The men turned their faces again towards the camp; their hearts were heavy and their thoughts were sad.

To this day the rocks remain between Double Island Point and Inship Point, When a rainbow appears in the sky, the old men of the tribe tell the story of the disobedience and punishment of the wandering boys.

MIRRAGAN, THE FISHERMAN

A Tale of the Wollandilly River, Whambeyan and Jenolan Caves.

NOTE.--The Jenolan are wonderful subterranean caves of limestone formation, situated in the Blue Mountains, New South Wales. They are set in the midst of wild and rugged mountain scenery, where rivers wind away like silver ribbons to the distant sea, and the mountain kings are crowned with snow. In these deep, mysterious caves of crystalline wonder Nature has surpassed herself in artistry.

Ages ago, in the dream-time, many of the animals now on earth were men. They were much bigger than the blackfellows of the present time, and were possessed of wonderful magic power, which allowed them to move mountains, make rivers, and perform many other feats of extraordinary strength and daring. At this time, Gurangatch lived in a very deep waterhole at the junction of what we now know as the Wollondilly and Wingeecaribee Rivers, in New South Wales. Gurangatch was half fish and half reptile, with shimmering scales of green, purple and gold. His eyes shone like two bright stars through the clear green water of his camping ground. At mid-day, when the sun was high, he basked in the shallow water of the lagoon, and at nightfall retired to the dark depths of the pool.

Mirragan, the tiger-cat, was a famous fisherman. He would never trouble to trap or spear small fish, but would wait for the largest and most dangerous. One day he was passing by the waterhole, when he caught a glimpse of the gleaming eyes of Gurangatch. Instantly he threw a spear at him, but Gurangatch swam to the bottom of the waterhole, which was very deep. Mirragan sat on the bank for some time, and wondered how he could catch such a splendid fish. At last he hit upon a plan. He went into the bush and cut a lot of bark, carried it to the waterhole, and placed it under the water at several positions around the bank. He intended to poison the water with the bark, and thus cause Gurangatch to rise to the surface. The water made Gurangatch very sick, but it was not sufficiently poisonous to cause him to rise to the surface. After waiting for a considerable time, Mirragan realised that his plan had failed. He was sorely disappointed, but again went in search of more bark.

When Gurangatch saw his enemy depart, he suspected some other trick. In order to escape, he commenced to tear up the ground for many miles, and the water of the lagoon flowed after him. In this manner he formed the present valley of the Wollondilly River. He then burrowed underground for several miles, and came out on the side of the valley by a high rocky ridge, which is now known as the Rocky Waterhole. When Gurangatch reached this lagoon, he raised his head and put out his tongue, which flashed like summer lightning across a stormy sky. From this vantage place he saw Mirragan following swiftly in his trail. Gurangatch then re turned along his burrow to the Wollondilly, and continued to make a channel for himself. When he arrived at the junction of the Guineacor River, he turned to the left and continued its course for a few miles. At last he arrived at a very rocky place, which was hard to burrow through. He therefore turned on his track and continued his former course, which is the long bend in the Wollondilly at this point. He then made Jock's Creek-which flows into the Wollondilly-and, on reaching its source, he again burrowed deep beneath the mountain ranges, and came up inside the Whambeyan Caves.

Let us now return to the adventures of Mirragan. When he arrived at the waterhole with the second load of bark, he saw that Gurangatch had escaped. He then following him many miles down the river, until he overtook him at the Whambeyan Caves. Mirragan was afraid to follow Gurangatch along the dark underground passages of the caves. He now climbed on top of the rocks and dug a very deep hole, and then poked a pole down as far as it would reach in order to frighten Gurangatch out of his safe retreat. However, he did not succeed with the first, hole, and so he made many of them. These holes still remain on the top of Whambeyan Caves.

One morning, at daybreak, Gurangatch escaped through his tunnel to the Wollondilly again. Now, Mirragan's family lived a few miles down the river and, when they saw Gurangatch coming, with the water roaring and seething after him like a great river in flood, they were terrified, and ran up the side of the mountain for safety. At this time Mirragan appeared on the scene of trouble, and his wife upbraided him for disturbing Gurangatch, and begged him to leave his enemy in peace. Mirragan listened very patiently, but would not be dissuaded. He again took up the relentless chase, and overtook Gurangatch at a place called Slippery Rock. Here they fought a desperate fight, until they made the rock quite smooth with their struggles-hence its name. After fighting for some time, Gurangatch escaped and continued his course. The water flowed after him in a roaring torrent. Mirragan followed, and, every time he overtook his enemy, he struck him with a heavy club, while Gurangatch retaliated by striking him with his tail.

This battle continued down the course of Cox's River to the junction of Katoomba Creek. He then doubled on his course, and again travelled up the Cox. Mirragan was close on his trail, and, in order to escape, he again burrowed underground, and came out on Mouin Mountain. Here he made a very deep waterhole, which, even to the present day, is a danger to cattle, on account of its depth. After much travelling he at last arrived at Jenolan Caves, where he met many of his relations. Gurangatch was tired and weary from his long journey, and very sore from the blows he had received. Turning to his relations, he said: "I am weary and very sore; many days have I travelled, and many nights have I watched the moon rise over the mountains and again sink beneath the earth. My enemy continues to hunt me, and will surely kill me. Take me, O my brothers, to a dark, deep waterhole that lies beyond the mountains, and I will rest." They then took him from the eaves to a waterhole beyond the mountain ranges.

Mirragan was very tired when he arrived at Binnoomur,

so he rested himself on a hill. When he had regained his strength, he searched about the caves and saw the tracks of Gurangatch and his relations, and the direction they had taken to the waterhole. Being very tired, he decided that the best thing to do was to seek his own friends and ask their help. Mirragan then travelled far to the west, where the camping ground of his friends was set. On reaching their camp he found them eating roasted eels. They offered him a portion, but he said: "I do not want such little things. I have been hunting a great fish for many days and nights. His eyes shine like stars when the night is cold, and his body shimmers like the noonday sun. His friends have taken him over the mountains to the Joolundoo waterhole. Will you send the best divers in the camp with me so that we may kill him?" After much consideration they decided to send Billagoola the Shag, Goolagwangwan the Diver, Gundhareen the Black Duck, and Goonarring the Wood Duck.

When Mirragan and his comrades arrived at the waterhole in which Gurangatch was hiding, Gundhareen the Black Duck preened his feathers and dived into the waterhole. He quickly returned and said, "There is no bottom to the hole." The others laughed, and Goolagwangwan the Diver said: "I will teach you how to dive; there is no waterhole in the land I cannot fathom." After a while he returned with a small fish and said, "Is this the enemy you were seeking?" Mirragan grew very angry, and replied, "No! It is too small." Billagoola the Shag made the next attempt, and when he had descended a long way he saw a shoal of small fish trying to hide Gurangatch by covering him over with mud. Billagoola made a desperate effort to seize Gurangatch, but it was impossible, as he was fast in the crevice of a rock. Billagoola returned to the surface and again dived. This time he tore a great piece of flesh out of the back of Gurangatch. When Mirragan saw the flesh, he was delighted, and exclaimed, "This is a piece of the fish I have hunted many days and nights."

A camp fire was started and the meat cooked. After they had eaten it, Mirragan and his friends returned to their camps across the mountains.

And this is how the Wollondilly, Cox and Guineacor Rivers, the Whambeyan and Jenolan Caves were formed. Whenever you visit those wonderful caves, you will remember the resting-place of Gurangatch, the star-eyed, and when you see the "pot-holes" on the top of Whambeyan Caves, you will be reminded of the work of Mirragan, the Relentless.

HOW FIRE WAS STOLEN FROM THE
RED-CRESTED COCKATOO

Ages ago--in the dream-time--many of the beautiful birds and timid animals now living in the bush were men. One day, towards sunset, a tribe of blacks were returning from the hunt, when they met a very old man carrying a long spear and an empty "dilly" bag. When he approached them he placed the spear in the ground as a token of peace, and said: "I have travelled far, my brothers, and many moons have gone since I left the hunting ground of my people. I have journeyed to the land where the voice of the great waters is like rolling thunder. I have passed beyond the mountains that are hidden in grey mist to the great red plains beyond, where there is neither bird nor beast, and the face of the sun is for ever hidden in a dark cloud. I have journeyed without resting to the land. that lies beyond the dawn, and many strange adventures have I known. Now I am old, and my people are scattered like dead leaves before the wind, and, before I seek them, I would rest with you a while. In return for your kindness, I will tell you the secret of the fire of the sun. He who is brave among you may then bring it to your tribe."

The headmen of the tribe decided to take the old man with them to their camping ground. When they arrived the evening meal was quickly prepared, and the choicest morsels were given to the weary traveller. The blacks then formed a circle around the old man, and eagerly awaited his story. At this time fire was unknown in the land. When the blacks enjoyed the warmth of the sun, they often wondered how they could take the fire from the sky in order to warm them when the snow fell like a great white mantle, and the cold wind howled eerily and chilled them to the bone. They did not know how to cook their food or harden their spear heads by fire, but for warmth alone they desired it. The old man crouched on his haunches, wrapped his possum skin rug around him, peered into the darkness of the bush as though he suspected a hidden enemy, and, having made himself comfortable, began to tell of his adventurous journey.

"Far to the east, beyond the mountains that hide the sun, I journeyed," he said. "The water no longer ran in the creeks, and the waterholes were dry. Many animals were dead in the bed of the river, to which they had come for water, and died from thirst. The shadow of death was across the land, and I hurried on without resting, lest it should fall across my path. One day, when my tongue was big in my mouth, and my legs were as weak as those of a child, I saw in the distance a gleaming waterhole. I ran towards it, but fell, many times before reaching it, so great was my weakness. At last I reached it, but the blackness of night fell upon me, and I slept, although the sun was high in the sky. When I awoke I heard a loud noise in my ears like the buzzing of many flies, and my legs would not support me. I dragged myself to the waterhole, and, bending my head low to drink, I touched the hot, dry sand with my mouth. That which I thought was water was a gleaming bed of sand. An evil spirit possessed me, and I dug deep into the sand until my hands were torn and bleeding. The sand became firmer, and at last a trickle of water appeared. It gradually increased until there was sufficient for me to drink. I rested there for a day, and then went on my way refreshed. After many days, I came to a land where grew many high trees. One morning, before the sun had climbed the mountains, I saw its fire gleaming through the trees. Being surprised at the sight, I cautiously drew nearer, and then I saw Mar-the Cockatoo-take the fire from under his crest and light his way with it. In my hurry I stood on a dry stick, and its crackling drew the cockatoo's attention to me. He threw a spear at me, and I was forced to flee. After many weary days and nights, I arrived at the camping ground of my people, but they were no longer there. Then I followed in their tracks until I met you. If there is one among your tribe who is brave enough to face the dangers of my long and weary journey, and take the fire from Mar, the cockatoo, then his name shall be a welcome word on all men's tongues until the end of time."

When they heard this story, the tribe were greatly excited. They all spoke together, and few were heard. At last they agreed to invite the cockatoo to a great corroboree, and, while he was enjoying himself, to steal the fire. The day arrived for the great feast. There was dancing and singing, and mock fighting. Then they offered Mar a choice piece of kangaroo flesh to eat, but he refused it. He was then offered the kangaroo skin, which he accepted and took away with him to his camp. The f east was over, and still they did not have the fire.

Prite, who was a very little fellow, decided to follow the cockatoo to his camp. He followed Mar over the mountains until he was very weary, and, just as he was about to turn back, he saw the cockatoo take the fire from under his crest feathers. He then returned to the camp and told the members of the tribe that the old man's story was true. The absorbing question was discussed late into the night, and at length it was agreed that Tatkanna, the Robin, should make the journey again, and endeavor to steal the coveted fire. Early the next morning he set out on his long journey, and, after travelling for some time, he reached the camp of the cockatoo. He arrived just in time to see Mar take the fire from his crest and light a fire stick. With this stick he singed off the hair of the kangaroo skin which the tribe had given him.

Tatkanna was so eager to steal the fire that he approached too close, and scorched his breast feathers-hence his name Robin Redbreast. When Tatkanna's feathers were scorched he was very frightened, but, as the cockatoo had seen him, he decided to act boldly. Running to the fire, he seized a fire stick and made off. In his hurry he set fire to the dry grass around him, and in a short time the whole bush was ablaze. The fire roared like the sound of flood waters in the mountains. Birds and animals raced before it in their efforts to gain the shelter of the green trees. But it swept all before it, and left a smoking black waste behind. When a tall tree fell, a shower of golden sparks flew high in the air, and the red reflection of the flames in the sky was like the rising of the sun.

When the cockatoo discovered that the fire was stolen, and beyond his control for all time, he was very angry. Taking his nulla-nullas, he went in search of Tatkanna to kill him. When Mar arrived at the camping ground of the tribe, Tatkanna, who was only a little fellow, was very frightened, and begged his friend Quartang, the Kookaburra, to take up his quarrel. Quartang agreed to do so, but he had not been fighting many minutes when he was beaten, and forced to fly into the trees, where he has remained ever since. Mar, the cockatoo, returned to his camp disconsolate. The tribe was very pleased with the robin for his bravery. When you see a red-crested cockatoo, you will remember how fire was stolen from him. He still has a beautiful red crest, and is known as Leadbeater's cockatoo. The robin redbreast also retains his scorched feathers in remembrance of his great feat.

WHY THE FISH-HAWK WAS
DRIVEN TO THE SEA

One day a Fish-hawk decided to catch some fish in a waterhole close to his camping ground. He gathered some bitter bark in the bush and placed it in the water. He knew that the bitter taste of the water would make the fish sick, and they would float to the surface and be easily speared. Having arranged the layers of bark in the water, he went to sleep beneath the shade of a tree for a little while. But a pheasant happened to be passing that way, and noticed the fish floating in the water. He therefore quickly took the opportunity of spearing them.

When the hawk returned, he met the pheasant carrying a string of fish tied to a bundle of spears. "Those are nice fish you have," remarked the hawk. "Where did you catch them?"

"They were floating in the waterhole, and I speared them," replied the pheasant.

The hawk claimed the fish as his property, but the pheasant only laughed at him and said: "You did not poison the fish. When I passed you were asleep in the shade of a tree. You cannot sleep and catch fish at the same time."

The hawk was very annoyed, and determined to be revenged for the mean trick played on him. One day he watched the pheasant place his spears on the bank of a river while he set some fish traps. The hawk crept along cautiously, and, stealing the spears, hid them in the branches of a tall tree. When the pheasant returned, he discovered his loss, and began to search for the missing spears. He saw the tracks of the hawk in the sand, and, following them, came to the tree in which the spears were hidden. The marks on the trunk of the tree made by the axe used in climbing directed him to the branch, and there he recovered his lost spears.

The hawk did not think of waiting to see the pheasant return, but went to his camp in high glee at the thought of the trick he had served the pheasant. Some time later the pheasant passed his camp with a string of big fish tied to a bundle of spears. The hawk was surprised at the sight of the spears, but determined to follow the pheasant and steal them again. When the pheasant reached his camp, he lit a fire and prepared his evening meal. After he had eaten it, he nodded drowsily by the fire, and in a short time was asleep. The hawk crept from his hiding-place, and again stole the bundle of spears. He then searched until he found a very tall tree, and, climbing it, placed the spears in the fork of the highest branch. When the pheasant awoke, he discovered the loss of his spears, but it was not long before he found traces of the hawk in the bush close to the camp. He followed the tracks for a long distance through the bush, but lost them in the thick undergrowth. After searching long into the night, he at last found the tree in which they were hidden, but he was too lazy to climb for them. He then travelled over the mountains until he reached the source of the river that flowed into the waterhole in which the hawk fished. The pheasant was possessed of magical powers, so he caused a flood at the head of the river that swept down the mountain side, and drove all the fish and the fish-hawk into the sea. Since that time the fish-hawk has been forced to live along the coast, and eat no other food but fish.

The pheasant returned to his camp when he had settled with his enemy, but he had no spears. He again set out to find the tree in which they were hidden. The flood had swept away all traces of the hawk's tracks, and his search was fruitless. He travelled again to the mountains in search of a tall tree with foot holes cut in the bark. He found a number of trees with such marks, and was forced to climb all of them in search of the missing spears. his efforts were, however, unrewarded. The pheasant never found his bundle of spears. In the bush you will see him flying from branch to branch in the tall trees. He is still searching for the stolen spears.

HOW THE NATIVE BEAR
LOST HIS TAIL

———————

The native bear and the whip-tail kangaroo were very friendly. They shared the same gunyah, and hunted together, and were very proud of their long tails. At this time a drought was over the land. Water was very scarce, and the two friends had camped by a shallow waterhole which contained some stagnant water. It was very nauseating to have to drink such water after the clear springs of the mountains. Nevertheless, it saved them from dying of thirst. At sunset banks of dark clouds would float low across the sky, and give promise of heavy rain, but at sunrise the sky would be as bright and clear as before, At last even the supply of stagnant water was exhausted, and the two friends were in a desperate plight.

After some time the kangaroo spoke and said: "When my mother carried me in her pouch I remember such a drought as this. The birds fell from the trees, the animals died fighting around dry waterholes, and the trees withered and died. My mother travelled far with me, over the mountains and down by the river bed, but she travelled slowly, as hunger and thirst had made her very weak, and I was heavy to carry. Then another kangaroo spoke to her and said: 'Why do you carry such a heavy burden? You will surely die. Throw him into the bush and come with me, for I will travel fast and take you to water.' My mother would not leave me to die, but struggled on, and the other kangaroo left her to die from thirst. Wearied by her heavy burden, she struggled on until she again came to a sandy river bed. She now dug a deep hole in the sand, which slowly filled with cool, clear water. We camped by this waterhole until the rain came. I shall go to the river and see if I can dig and find water, for if we stay here we shall surely perish from thirst."

The native bear was delighted at the suggestion, and said: "Yes! Let us both go down to the river bed. I have very strong arms, and will help you." They made their way to the river, but, before reaching it, stumbled across some of their friends who had died of thirst. This made them very serious and determined. When they reached the river, the sun was very hot and they were very tired. The native bear suggested that the kangaroo should start digging, as he knew most about it. The kangaroo went to work with a will, and dug a deep hole, but no signs of water were visible. The kangaroo was exhausted with his work, and asked the native bear to help him. The native bear was very cunning, and said: "I would willingly help you, but I am feeling very ill; the sun is very hot, and I am afraid I am going to die." The kangaroo was very sorry for his friend, and set to work again without complaining.

At last his work was rewarded. A trickle of water appeared in the bottom of the hole, and gradually increased until it filled it to overflowing. The kangaroo went over to his friend, and, touching him gently on the shoulder, said: "I have discovered water, and will bring some to you." But the native bear was only shamming, and dashed straight to the waterhole without even replying to the surprised kangaroo. When the native bear bent down to drink the water his tail stuck out like a dry stick. The kangaroo, who could now see the despicable cunning of his friend, was very angry, and, seizing his boomerang, cut off the tail of the drinker as it projected above the waterhole. To this day the native bear has no tail as an evidence of his former laziness and cunning.